AF615621

DATE DUE

5-26			
APR 1			
NOV 6			

CHERRY CREEK DIST. #5
PRAIRIE MEDIA CENTER
12600 E. JEWELL AVENUE
AURORA, COLORADO 80012

R01132 63600

Censorship

Censorship

by Melvin Berger

Franklin Watts
New York / London / Toronto / Sydney / 1982
an Impact Book

R01132 63600

Photographs courtesy of The Free Library of Philadelphia: pp. 3 (both) and 11; The Bettmann Archive, Inc.: pp. 5, 19, and 66; Culver Pictures, Inc.: pp. 6, 10 (both); United Press International: pp. 36 and 56.

Cartoons courtesy of Rothco: pp. 40 (Blaine/*The Spectator*, Hamilton, Canada), 63 (Taylor/*Albuquerque Tribune*, New Mexico), 71 (Miller/*News & Observer*, Raleigh, North Carolina), 74 (Pierotti).

Library of Congress Cataloging in Publication Data

Berger, Melvin.
Censorship.

(An Impact book)
Bibliography: p.
Includes index.
Summary: Presents the history of censoring information in the western world and discusses issues, as well as some specific cases, involving obscenity, libel, espionage, pornography, and student rights.
1. Censorship. [1. Censorship] I. Title.
Z657.B495 363.3'1 82-4754
ISBN 0-531-04483-1 AACR2

Copyright © 1982 by Melvin Berger
All rights reserved
Printed in the United States of America
5 4 3 2 1

363 .31 B453ce
Berger, Melvin.
Censorship /

Contents

Censorship

Chapter One

The Language of Censorship

Censorship is the control of communication between people. It includes restrictions on what can be written in books, newspapers, and magazines; what can be shown in movies and plays and on television; and what can be said in speeches and on radio. Mostly, censorship is practiced by governments. But religious and political leaders and special-interest groups also sometimes try to control the flow of information.

The word *censor* comes from the Latin, *censere*, which means "to count," as well as "to assess" or "estimate." The first censors were two well-respected government officials, appointed to conduct a census in ancient Rome in the year 443 B.C. Their duties were to count and register all the citizens, and to determine the value of each citizen's property. Taxes were then levied according to the censor's estimate.

The Roman censors also presided at the Tribunal of Fame. Here they paid honor to the citizens whom they found had performed noble or virtuous deeds. At the same time, they barred from public life anyone who had violated the accepted rules of conduct. Once both censors agreed on a position, their power to punish wrongdoers was unrestrained. The office of censor continued until the end of the Roman Empire.

From the Greeks to the Middle Ages

The idea of censorship was accepted even before the word censor came into being. The officials of ancient Greece, for example, had a high regard for freedom of religion and freedom of speech. But they refused to allow the free expression of opinions that went against the state religion. They feared that the gods would be angered, and this might bring harm to the people of Greece.

Socrates (470?–399 B.C.), the great Greek philosopher, devoted his life to a search for truth and goodness. He considered it his duty to awaken the people of his city of Athens to the need for wisdom and knowledge. His method was to question his listeners about their beliefs as a way of helping them to go beyond mere opinion to the discovery of essential truths.

Not everyone in Athens approved of Socrates' teaching method. Several rulers of the city accused him of showing disrespect for the gods, corrupting the morals of the young by leading them away from the old religion, popularizing science in a way that led to doubt and unbelief, and deceiving by trickery. The great thinker was brought to trial and found guilty of degrading public morals. He was sentenced to death by drinking a cup of the poison hemlock, making him the first known victim of censorship.

From those early times, too, come other clues about the power of the censors. In his play *Ion*, the Greek dramatist Euripides (480?–406 B.C.), whose ideas were not always accepted by the politicians of his time, has his hero pray, "may free speech be mine." And in the following century, the orator Demosthenes (384–322 B.C.), best known for his speeches in favor of Greek freedom, declared that the worst

Above: the death of Greek philosopher Socrates, 470?–399 B.C.
Below: Euripides, Greek dramatist, 480?–406 B.C.

fate that could strike a people is "the deprivation of free speech."

The practice of censorship continued through the Middle Ages. The religious and government censors during these centuries had few misgivings about completely suppressing views with which they disagreed. They vigorously protected church and state from any verbal or written attack. The Roman Catholic Church considered heresy the most grievous of all crimes. Heresy is the expression of opinions or ideas that go against the accepted doctrines; people found guilty of heresy are called heretics. The Christian Church punished heretics with exile, torture, or death.

In England, the struggle for free speech and a free press was especially strong. From the English Parliament in 1275 came the earliest censorship statute. It outlawed "any false news or tales whereby discord or occasion of discord or slander may grow between the King and his people. . . ." The punishment for anyone violating this law was set by the King's Council sitting in the so-called Star Chamber.

The freedom of printers and writers to publish whatever they like has been debated since the invention of printing in the 1400s. The first known system of book licensing was instituted in England the following century. The aim of the system was the suppression of "certain seditious and heretical books." A seditious book is one that incites rebellion against the government.

Licensing is one of the oldest ways of censoring or restraining the press. It requires a publisher to obtain a formal license from the government in advance of publication. If officials find the material objectionable, they merely do not grant the license, and the book or paper cannot be printed.

The atmosphere of the times restricted freedom of speech and the press in regard to politics and religion. But the portrayal of unrestrained sexual conduct was still commonly accepted. People of all classes enjoyed books, plays, songs, and artwork that, by today's standards, would be considered lewd and coarse. No one considered these materials to be indecent or offensive. It was not until much later that censorship began to focus on sexual content.

Galileo Galilei, Italian astronomer, 1564–1642. He is depicted here in prison being visited by John Milton, the author of *Paradise Lost*. Galileo was tried for heresy for his belief that the earth orbits the sun and not vice versa.

Influence of Puritanism

Puritan religious beliefs were first expressed in England in the late 1500s. In an effort to "purify" their religion, the Puritans set for themselves a very strict moral code. They tried to realize fully God's will, both in their worship and in their day-to-day behavior. As Puritanism became more widespread, they attempted to get rid of all purely pleasurable activities, which they considered sinful and immoral. They labeled certain books as "wanton workes," and condemned particular behaviors.

One famous case in June 1663, which involved Sir Charles Sedley, a friend of King Charles II of England, shows the influence of Puritanism. Sedley had been drinking too much at a tavern in London and became thoroughly drunk. He climbed to a balcony of the establishment, threw off all his clothes, swore and cursed at the crowd that had gathered below, and then, in a fury, poured urine from bottles down on their heads.

During the riot that followed, Sir Charles was arrested, tried, and found guilty of obscene behavior. He was fined 2,000 marks. His case is often cited as the first known instance of a conviction based on a charge of obscenity. From then until now, obscenity has been defined as any expression that stirs the sexual impulse and leads to unacceptable sexual thoughts. The word comes from the Latin, *ob*—towards, and *caenum*—dirt or filth.

Another important censorship case arose in England the same year as the Sedley case. William Twyn was arrested and found guilty of printing a seditious book that endorsed the

Sir Charles Sedley, British dramatist and wit, 1639?–1701. Sedley was found guilty of obscene behavior and fined 2,000 marks. His is the first known instance of a conviction based on an obscenity charge.

people's right of revolution. His punishment was particularly brutal. He was hung. But then, just before dying, he was cut down, beheaded, and quartered. It is easy to imagine the effect this must have had on others who wanted to criticize the government!

During the 1700s, many obscenity cases were tried in England. One of the better known involved a man named Read who wrote a book entitled, *The Fifteen Plagues of a Maidenhead*. The court described it as "bawdy stuff," but insisted that it was "punishable only in the spiritual court." It did not belong in a court of law, since it was neither anti-religious nor anti-government. According to the official position, if a publication did not threaten either the church or government, there seemed to be no limit to the amount of explicit sexual material it could contain.

The American Colonies

The colonization of America began in the seventeenth century as increasing numbers of people came to our shores from England and other countries of Europe. The colonies were governed by the laws of England. One set of censorship laws had to do with defamation, which is an attack on someone's good name or reputation. Defamation can either be written, which is libel, or spoken, which is slander.

Curiously enough, truth was no defense in cases of defamation. For example, if someone accused a government official of dishonesty, and proved the claim, the person was still considered guilty of libel or slander. Also, the jury that sat in trials of those accused of violating these censorship laws could only decide whether or not the person had written or spoken the statement in question. It was then up to the judge alone to decide if the words were libelous or slanderous, and if guilty, to fix the punishment.

Other forms of censorship were also practiced in the colonies. The first book burning in America was performed by the public executioner in the chief marketplace of Boston. The book was Thomas Pynchon's *The Meritorious Price of Our Redemption*. According to the censor, it stated religious ideas that differed from those of the colony.

Newspaper suppression also originated in Boston. On September 25, 1690, Benjamin Harris started publication of *Publick Occurrences Both Foreign and Domestic*, and the governor immediately closed it down. First of all, Harris had published without the license required by the Massachusetts colony. Then, he had included articles telling how the Indian allies of the British in the war against the French had not joined in a crucial battle. And finally, he had described the King of France's affair with his daughter-in-law. This last item was thought to be much too risqué for a decent publication.

Another challenge to freedom of the press occurred in 1722. James Franklin, publisher of Boston's *New England Courant*, was jailed because he printed an article that criticized the government for not protecting shipping against pirate attack. While James Franklin was serving his one-month prison sentence, his younger brother, Ben, took over the paper. Although Ben Franklin did not continue to find fault with the authorities, he did print the famous statement, "Whoever would overthrow the liberty of a nation must begin by subduing the freeness of speech."

The most important and most famous censorship case in colonial America took place in 1735. John Peter Zenger (1697–1746), the printer, editor, and publisher of the *New York Weekly Journal*, was accused of writing articles highly critical of the British governor, William Cosby. Zenger reported that the governor had influenced the outcome in court cases, had tampered with election results, and had showed favoritism in his political appointments. As a result, Zenger was arrested and put on trial for seditious libel.

At first the judge, Chief Justice De Lancy, a strong supporter of the governor, suspended Zenger's lawyers. The publisher was left without legal protection. But then Andrew Hamilton, a noted Philadelphia lawyer, came to Zenger's aid. Hamilton told the court that since the writer had only printed the truth, he was innocent of any wrongdoing. The truth, Hamilton maintained, is not libelous.

Up until then, according to English and American common law, the truth had been no defense against libel, and the

THE

New-York Weekly JOURNAL

Containing the freshest Advices, Foreign, and Domestick.

MUNDAY November 25*th*, 1734.

***To all my Subscribers and Benefactors wvo take my weekly* Journall.**

Gentlemen, Ladies and Others;

AS you last week were Disappointed of my Journall, I think it Incumbent upon me, to publish my Apoligy which is this. On the Lords Day, the Seventeenth of this Instant, I was Arrested, taken and Imprisoned in the common Goal of this Citty, by Virtue of a Warrant from the *Governour*, and the Honorable *Francis Harrison*, Esq; and others in Councill of which (God willing) yo'l have a Coppy, whereupon I was put under such Restraint that I had not the Liberty of Pen, Ink, or Paper, or to see, or speak with People, till upon my Complaint to the Honourable the Chief Justice, at my appearing before him upon my *Habias Corpus* on the *Wednesday* following. Who discountenanced that Proceeding, and therefore I have had since that Time, the Liberty of Speaking through the Hole of the Door, to my Wife and Servants by which I doubt not yo'l think me sufficiently Excused for not sending my last weeks *Journall*, and I hope for the future by the Liberty of Speaking to my Servants thro' the Hole of the Door of the Prison, to entertain you with my weekly *Journal* as formerly.

And am your obliged
Humble Servant,
J. Peter Zenger.

Mr. *Zenger*;

AS the Liberty of the Press is justly esteemed and universally acknowledged by Englishmen, to be the grand Paladium of all their Liberties, which Liberty of the Press, I have rejoyced to see well defended in Sundry of your Papers, and particularly by your No. 2. 3. 10. 11. 15. 16. 17. 18. 24. & 54. and by an annoninous Authors Observations on the chief Justices Charge of *January* last; now, for as much as it may not only be of present Use, but of future Advantage, that such Matters of Fact, that concern the Liberty of the Press, may be faithfully recorded and transmitted to Posterity, therefore I have sent you a Detail of such particulars that concern the Liberty of the Press within this Colony, and because I would not have you or my self charged with the Publication of a Libel, I shall confine my self to a plain Narration of Facts without any comments.

On Tuesday *the* 15*th of* Octo. 1734. *The supream Court of* New-York, *began, when the Honourable* James De Lancey, Esq; *Cheif Justie charged the Grand Jury. The Conclusion of which Charge was as follows.*

Gentlemen, I shall conclude with reading a Paragraph or two out of the same Book, † concerning Libels; they are arrived to that height, that they call

Top left: a page from John Peter Zenger's *Weekly Journal* containing the editor's defense of his actions and freedom of the press. Bottom left: the burning of the *Weekly Journal* by the British. Above: a diorama of Zenger's libel trial, with Andrew Hamilton acting as his atttorney.

jury's role had merely been to decide whether or not the defendant had made the statement. The brilliance of Hamilton's words, though, convinced the jury to consider the truth of Zenger's accusations and whether or not they were libelous.

The jury found that Zenger had indeed told the truth. Therefore, he was not guilty of libel. The verdict established the all-important principle that the truth is a defense against libel, and that the jury has the right to decide if a particular statement is libelous.

The U.S. Constitution

When Congress voted to accept the Constitution in 1789, many people expressed concern over the omission of guaranteed human rights. Justice Hugo L. Black of the U.S. Supreme Court, in writing a 1971 decision, described the situation this way:

> *When the Constitution was adopted, many people strongly opposed it because the document contained no Bill of Rights to safeguard certain basic freedoms. They especially feared that the new powers granted to a central government might be interpreted to permit the government to curtail freedom of religion, press, assembly, and speech. In response to an overwhelming public clamor, James Madison offered a series of amendments to satisfy citizens that these great liberties would remain safe and beyond the power of government to abridge.*

On December 15, 1791, the first ten Amendments, known as the Bill of Rights, were approved and made a permanent part of the Constitution. The First Amendment is central to any discussion of censorship. It reads as follows:

> *Congress shall make no law respecting an establishment of religion, or prohibiting the free exercise thereof;* or abridging the freedom of speech, or of the

press; *or of the right of the people peaceably to assemble, and to petition the Government for a redress of grievances. (Emphasis added.)*

Some thinkers take the words of the First Amendment literally. It is their view that government should be absolutely prohibited from censoring or in any other way controlling the freedom of speech and of the press. Others say that there are certain circumstances, such as cases of obscenity, libel, or treason, when it is proper to restrain these freedoms.

American courts and political leaders have long struggled with the basic question of censorship. During some periods, such as in times of war, the public mood is inclined toward control and suppression, and censorship is widely practiced and accepted. At other times, the nation is more concerned with protecting individual freedoms, and all attempts at censorship are strongly resisted.

The First Amendment of the Constitution is the very touchstone of our democracy. That is why the issue of control of expression is of the greatest importance to all of us. A well-informed citizenry is the best safeguard of the liberty of all. It is also the strongest guarantee for the future of our nation.

Chapter Two

Obscenity vs. Morality

"This book is full of filth and smut."
"It is not. It is a serious work of art."

"These pictures are harmful for children to see."
"Words or pictures can never hurt anyone."

"The movie is offensive and disgusting. It should be banned."
"If you don't approve, don't go to see it."

"There should be a law against this kind of trash."
"In a democracy I can read whatever I want."

"Children get antisocial ideas from violence on TV."
"Then parents should not let their kids watch TV."

The arguments for and against the censorship of obscenity in books, magazines and newspapers, on TV, and in the movies are familiar. They have raged long and hard. Yet neither the length, nor heat, of the controversy has changed the views of either side.

Throughout history, the reactions to obscenity have see-sawed—now sternly prosecuting the makers of even slightly off-color remarks, now ignoring the most explicit sexual references. The results have ranged widely, too, from the vote of the school board in Cedar Lakes, Indiana, to remove the *American Heritage Dictionary* from the high school library because it contained "39 dirty words," to the open sale of obscene books and sexual materials in the downtown districts of many American cities.

Censorship of obscenity is a relatively new concept; it is only about three hundred years old. The earliest cases date back to the seventeenth century, when literacy spread among the masses. As reading extended from the upper classes and clergy to the rest of the citizenry, those in power acted to prevent publication of any material they considered objectionable. At first they imposed censorship by insisting on the strict licensing of all printed matter before publication. In time, the licensing laws were struck down. Then new laws were enacted making it a crime to publish or distribute anything judged to be obscene.

The early cases of obscenity tried in the United States were based largely on decisions that had been made in the English courts. The first obscenity trial on record took place in Philadelphia in 1815. Jesse Sharpless and his associates were found guilty of charging people to view a painting "representing a man in an obscene, impudent and indecent posture with a woman."

The original case of a book being banned for obscenity took place just a few years later. Peter Holmes was convicted in Massachusetts for reprinting John Cleland's novel, *Fanny Hill*, an account of the life of a prostitute. When the novel first came out in England, around 1740, bookstore-owner Drybutter was placed in the pillory for offering the book for sale. In 1821, the Massachusetts court accused Holmes of "being a scandalous and evil disposed person," who was trying to debauch and corrupt the minds of the youths and other good citizens by publishing this "lewd, wicked, scandalous, infamous and obscene printed book." The judge found the book so awful, in fact, that he would not even allow the jury to see a copy. As a result, Holmes was found guilty of printing an obscene book by twelve men who had never even read one word!

The Courts Define Obscenity

An exact legal definition of obscenity is of the greatest importance in any consideration of censorship. In 1868, a case tried in Great Britain set the standard for the test of obscenity that lasted about a hundred years. The case involved Henry Scott, a metal broker in Wolverhampton, England. An outspoken anti-Catholic, Scott actively distributed books and pamphlets ridiculing the Pope and the Catholic Church. One pamphlet in particular made reference to sexual intimacies between priests and young women taking confession. Scott was arrested and charged with dispensing obscene literature.

The first court to hear the case found Scott guilty. On appeal, the decision was reversed, the judge declaring that Scott had not intended to be obscene. The Crown then appealed that verdict. Lord Chief Justice Cockburn in the higher court presented the definition of obscenity that prevailed in Great Britain and in the United States until quite recently:

> *I think the test of obscenity is this, whether the tendency of the matter charged as obscenity is to deprave and corrupt those whose minds are open to such immoral influence and into whose hands a publication of this sort may fall.*

In the remainder of his opinion, Cockburn made three important points that had a lasting impact in obscenity cases: A work may be suppressed if it deals with sexual matters, not only if it proves to be anti-government or anti-religious; the entire work is obscene, even if there is only a brief offensive passage; and a work is considered objectionable as long as it might corrupt the youngest and most susceptible members of society.

At about the same time the Cockburn decision went into effect in England, censorship activity was flaring up in the United States. Anthony Comstock (1844–1915), a grocery clerk in New York State, formed the Society for the Suppression of Vice. This organization was devoted to the strict enforcement of America's obscenity laws. The group goaded officials to enforce the state and federal anti-obscenity laws already on the books. It also pressured members of Congress to pass even stricter new laws.

Comstock and his committee were largely responsible for the major anti-obscenity legislation passed by Congress in 1873. This vigorous proponent of censorship once boasted that his investigations led to the arrest and conviction of nearly four hundred people, and that he personally destroyed 160 tons of obscene literature. His name lives on in our vocabulary; the word "comstockery" means overzealous censorship.

The moral tone Comstock set for the country lasted until around 1950. At that time, public pressure against the various obscenity laws began growing. In 1957, the test of the constitutionality of obscenity legislation finally came before the Supreme Court in the case *Roth v. United States*. Samuel Roth, a New York City businessman, employed fifteen workers selling erotic books, magazines, and photographs by mail. He claimed to have a mailing list of 40,000 and to have sent out about ten million items through the Post Office. Roth was charged with sending obscene material through the U.S. mail and was found guilty in a lower court.

The Supreme Court upheld Roth's conviction. Justice William J. Brennan Jr., stated that obscenity did not enjoy the protection of the First Amendment because obscenity is "utterly without redeeming social importance." The Court also made a distinction between sex and obscenity in this definition of obscenity: "Obscene material is material which deals with sex in a manner appealing to prurient interest."

The Court added the following words of explanation: "A thing is obscene if, considered as a whole, its predominant appeal is to prurient interest, i.e., a shameful or morbid interest in nudity, sex, or excretion, and if it goes beyond customary limits of candor in description or representation of such matters."

This decision was an attempt on the part of the Supreme Court to clear up the confusion on the exact definition of obscenity. Perhaps because the meaning was still unclear, dozens of cases continued to be tried in the courts. Most gave obscenity a very narrow interpretation. The Court's "prurient interest" yardstick became the constitutional test of obscenity. Only writing that was "without redeeming social importance" could be suppressed.

Tests of Obscenity Between 1959 and 1966

In 1959, a federal district court in New York issued a landmark obscenity decision. The case involved charges of obscenity against D. H. Lawrence's novel, *Lady Chatterley's Lover*. The court found the book was not obscene.

Judge Frederick van Pelt Bryan wrote the opinion:

> *These passages and this language understandably will shock the sensitive minded. Be that as it may, these passages are relevant to the plot and to the development of the characters and of their lives as Lawrence unfolds them.*

He continued:

> *The tests of obscenity are not whether the book or passages from it are in bad taste or shock or offend the sensibilities of an individual, or even a substantial segment of the community.*

The same argument was used in the flood of state-law suits that followed the 1961 publication in the United States of Henry Miller's novel, *Tropic of Cancer*, which he had written twenty-eight years earlier. Several state courts heard arguments over *Tropic of Cancer*, and the verdicts differed. Final-

English writer D. H. Lawrence, 1885–1930, author of the controversial *Lady Chatterley's Lover.*

ly, in 1964, the Supreme Court settled the case in favor of the book. It stated that the Miller work had artistic and literary value, and thus "social importance." For this reason, its contents were protected by the First Amendment.

Fanny Hill, the first book to be banned in the United States, came up again in a case before the Supreme Court in 1966. This time, one hundred forty-five years after it was first suppressed, the book was found not to be obscene. In arriving at its decision, the Court applied three tests to determine obscenity: Is it material without social value? Does its main theme appeal to prurient interest in sex? Is its representation of sexual matters an affront to contemporary community standards? On these bases, *Fanny Hill* was at last freed of all charges of obscenity.

With the *Fanny Hill* decision, many experts considered that literary censorship for obscenity reasons was done with for all time. Charles Rembar, the leading First Amendment lawyer who successfully defended *Fanny Hill*, *Lady Chatterley's Lover*, and *Tropic of Cancer*, wrote an account of these trials that he entitled, *The End of Obscenity*. In it he said, "So far as writers are concerned, there is no longer a law of obscenity." His conclusion, it now seems, was somewhat premature. The conflict was to continue on the local, state, and federal levels of government.

From 1967 to the Present

In 1967, the U.S. Congress decided to take a new look at the whole question of obscenity. They created a Commission on Obscenity and Pornography to study the problem and make recommendations. Its report, which was presented three years later to President Richard M. Nixon and the Congress, came to some surprising conclusions. The commission's chief recommendation to the Congress was that they "should not seek to interfere with the right of adults who wish to do so to read, obtain, or view explicit sexual materials." At the same time, they suggested regulating the sale of such materials to young people and insuring that such things should not be thrust on persons "without their consent through the mails or through open display. . . ."

The group stated its reasons for recommending that adults should be able to read and see anything they want. These included the following points: explicit sexual materials do not cause harm; they are sought by large numbers of individuals; public opinion opposes such restraints; prohibitions are hard to enforce; and it is unfair to limit adult communication to the level deemed suitable for children.

The report was soundly denounced and totally rejected by President Nixon and by a vote in the Senate.

By 1973, four new Nixon appointees were on the Supreme Court. It seemed an appropriate time for some new tests of the obscenity law. The first major decision came in the case of *Miller v. California*. Marvin Miller was accused and convicted under a California state law of sending obscene publications through the mail. Miller appealed. He claimed that the First Amendment made the California law unconstitutional.

By a 5 to 4 decision, the Court upheld Miller's conviction. In doing so, Chief Justice Warren E. Burger turned back Justice Brennan's earlier "social importance" test of obscenity. The new test was whether or not the entire work has any "serious literary, artistic, political or scientific value." Other criteria for obscenity were added to the list. For example, would an average person find that the work appeals to a prurient interest in sex? Does the work depict or describe sex in an objectionable way? Does it offend local community standards?

Justice William O. Douglas spoke for the four Justices who dissented in this case. He pointed out that no one is forced to read a book. Therefore, anyone who finds such materials offensive need never enter the stores where they are sold. Nor do they need to read a single page of the book in question. He also argued that parents and religious leaders, not the government, should protect children from harmful material. The definitions of obscenity are so vague, he also said, that it is wrong to punish people for violating laws that are impossible to understand or follow.

One of the first applications of the *Miller* ruling involved two sexually explicit magazines, *Screw* and *Smut*. Late in

1973, the postmaster general in Washington, D.C., directed four postal officials in small Kansas cities to order subscriptions to these magazines using fictitious names. Soon copies of the two New York publications began arriving in Kansas in plain, unmarked envelopes. The local postal officials sent the magazines on to the postmaster general.

Using the *Miller* decision, the Post Office then charged Al Goldstein, the publisher of the magazines, with twelve counts of obscenity in Kansas City because they were offensive to local community standards. Goldstein defended himself by saying that although he agreed that *Screw* was "tasteless and disgusting," it was not obscene. He was found guilty, but the verdict was later reversed on appeal.

Defenders of the First Amendment view the Goldstein case with dismay. They question whether it is proper for the government to prosecute obscenity cases in carefully chosen communities known to be conservative in their outlook and where the controversial publications are only available by mail. They think it gives a go-ahead signal to those who favor censorship, or at least desire some government control of the publications available to the public.

There is some evidence that a fear of more censorship to come is justified. Since 1974, over a thousand anti-obscenity bills have been introduced into state legislatures. At least twenty-six states have already passed anti-obscenity laws. The American Library Association has an Office for Intellectual Freedom to monitor book censorship issues. In the late 1970s, the office received about four complaints a week from librarians who were being pressed by various individuals or groups to remove certain books from the shelves. By 1981, the number had risen to four complaints a day.

In the past, would-be obscenity censors complained mostly about the "bad" language that was used and about explicit sexual content. Today, the main subjects of complaint are books dealing with homosexuality and sex education. They believe that reading such books contributes to socially undesirable behavior. Their goal, therefore, is to remove these books from libraries and schools and to prevent their sale in stores.

Those opposed to censorship object to the attempts of individuals or small groups to impose their views, standards, and tastes on others. Many of the arguments against censorship rest on the First Amendment's protection of freedom of expression. History shows, these citizens say, that once a government starts to impose censorship in any form, other protections under the law inevitably fall away, too.

Chapter Three

Libel vs. Individual Rights

"CAROL BURNETT AND HENRY K. IN ROW." This headline appeared in the March 2, 1976, edition of the *National Enquirer*, a top-selling gossip newspaper that specializes in uncovering scandals involving celebrities.

The article told how Carol Burnett, the well-known actress and comedian, had argued loudly with Henry Kissinger, former secretary of state, in a posh Washington, D.C., restaurant. It then described the way Miss Burnett had lurched drunkenly between the tables, offering everyone a bite of her dessert, and finally ended up spilling wine over one of the other diners.

Both Burnett and Kissinger insisted that there was no truth at all in the story, and the *Enquirer* did publish a brief retraction. But Burnett felt she had been portrayed as a rowdy drunk, and that the retraction did little to make up for the damage she had suffered.

Shortly after the story appeared, Burnett entered a $10 million suit against the *National Enquirer*. She sued them for libel, the legal term for false or untrue writings that injure a person's reputation or hold that person up to ridicule, hatred, or contempt.

It took five years for Burnett's case to come to trial. At

issue was whether the *Enquirer* had shown "actual malice" toward Burnett. In other words, did they publish the article knowing and not caring that it was false?

Burnett's case was largely based on the testimony of two restaurant employees who swore that they had told the paper, before publication, that the story was false. The *Enquirer* built its defense on the constitutional right of the press, under the First Amendment, to report all the news without restraint. "I speak," said the *Enquirer's* lawyer, " . . . for a principle, and that is the freedom of the press, your right to know."

On March 26, 1981, after a trial that lasted a little over a week, the jury awarded Carol Burnett $1.6 million in damages. Later, the amount was dropped to $800,000, though the *Enquirer* said it would appeal the decision. The sum is one of the largest damage awards ever granted in a libel case.

A number of newspaper people expressed approval of the trial's outcome. Reg Murphy, publisher of the *San Francisco Examiner*, for example, called the *Enquirer* "a disgrace to journalism," and said that they had not "played with the same rules" as other newspapers. But First Amendment lawyer Floyd Abrams was not too happy. He warned that such a large judgment could have bad effects. It might lead to many more suits against newspapers with ever-growing awards of money. This could possibly result in newspapers shying away from investigative reporting and truth-seeking, out of a fear of going bankrupt after losing just one libel decision.

Near v. Minnesota

The First Amendment states quite simply that Congress shall make no law abridging freedom of the press. But what exactly do these few words mean? Many court battles have been fought over the exact intention of this phrase. The 1931 case of *Near v. Minnesota* was one of the first to focus on the principle of press censorship.

Jay M. Near was one of the publishers of the *Saturday Press*, a weekly Minnesota scandal sheet. The paper was openly anti-Semitic and took every opportunity to level wild and unfounded accusations against the Jewish community.

One series of articles charged that Jewish gangsters controlled crime in the city. One particularly vicious passage read: "Practically every vendor of vile hooch, every owner of a moonshine still, every snake-faced gangster and embryonic yegg in the Twin Cities is a Jew. It is Jew, Jew, Jew, Jew, as long as one cares to comb over the records." What is more, the *Saturday Press* accused the police of being paid off by Jewish conspirators.

A Minnesota judge, on the basis of charges filed by a county attorney and under Minnesota's so-called Gag Law, ordered the paper to stop publishing. The law could be invoked against any "malicious, scandalous and defamatory" publication that was "a public nuisance." The case went up to the state's highest court, which found that the paper was indeed a nuisance and should be shut down.

Near, though, appealed the finding, and eventually the Supreme Court agreed to review the matter. In a 5 to 4 decision, the high Court struck down the Minnesota Gag Law for violating freedom of the press. The principle purpose of the First Amendment, Chief Justice Charles E. Hughes said, is "to prevent previous restraints upon publication." Of course, punishment after publication is possible, if it can be proved that a paper violated any obscenity or libel law. If Near libeled anyone, said Justice Hughes, then he can be sued *after* the article appears in print but not stopped from printing the article in the first place.

In his comments on the case, Hughes quoted James Madison concerning such abuses of freedom of the press as spreading lies and malicious scandals: "Some degree of abuse is inseparable from proper use of everything, and in no instance is this more true than in that of the press. . . . " In the opinion of Hughes, the First Amendment provides the press with absolute protection against censorship and particularly against prior restraint on publication.

The New York Times v. Sullivan

To win an award for libel today, a defendant, such as Carol Burnett in her suit against the *National Enquirer*, needs to prove "actual malice." This important doctrine came from the decision handed down by the Supreme Court in the 1964 case of *The New York Times v. Sullivan.*

In 1960, the civil rights movement was gaining strength in the Southern states. On March 29 of that year, *The New York Times* ran a full-page advertisement signed by sixty-four prominent individuals from many different fields. The ad charged that thousands of black students in Montgomery, Alabama, were facing "an unprecedented wave of terror" as they attempted to obtain their constitutional rights. It gave specific illustrations of cruel and punitive actions Montgomery police and others had taken against the students. Some of these points were later found to be in error.

L. B. Sullivan, city commissioner of Montgomery, sued the *Times* and four black Alabama clergymen who had signed the ad, for libel under the state of Alabama's civil defamation law. The suit claimed that some of the charges were false, and they defamed him as supervisor of the police department. The defendants were found guilty, and Sullivan was awarded $500,000 in damages. On appeal, the state court of Alabama affirmed the decision.

The New York Times decided to take the case to the Supreme Court. The central legal question to be decided was the constitutional protection for a public official in a libel action, as opposed to that of a private citizen. Justice William J. Brennan, Jr., took note of the Court's belief that "debate on political issues should be uninhibited, robust and wide-open, and that it may well include vehement, caustic and sometimes unpleasantly sharp attacks on government and public officials."

But what about the untrue statements in the ad? Said Brennan, "Erroneous statement is inevitable in free debate . . . it must be protected if the freedoms of expression are to have the 'breathing space' that they 'need to survive.'" In other words, the necessity to prove and substantiate every single criticism of a public official might have the effect of seriously limiting public debate.

Still, there remained the question of Sullivan's claim that

he had been defamed. Under what circumstances could he collect damages for libel?

In reply to this question, Brennan set an important new precedent for libel cases brought by public officials. A public official is prevented from recovering damages for an error relating to his conduct in office "unless he proves that the statement was made with 'actual malice'—that is, with knowledge that it was false or with reckless disregard of whether it was false or not."

The Supreme Court's decision in this case is considered to be very important because it affirms that it is the citizens' right, indeed their duty, to criticize the government. The opinion insists on proof of "actual malice" as the basis for a libel action, making it much harder for a public official to win such a suit. The decision became the first of a number of cases to define the laws of libel more strictly.

A few years after *The New York Times v. Sullivan* case, the Court handed down a decision that placed public figures in the same category as public officials. A public figure was defined as either someone actively involved in public affairs or who had gained fame or notoriety in some other way.

In *Gertz v. Robert Welch*, heard in 1974, the Supreme Court tried to differentiate between the requirements for winning a libel suit brought by a public official or public figure and one brought by a private citizen. Elmer Gertz was an attorney who was hired by a Chicago family to represent them in a civil suit against a policeman who had shot their son. An article in the March 1969 issue of *American Opinion*, published by Robert Welch's John Birch Society, claimed that Gertz was a "Leninist" and "Communist-fronter." The same publication also charged that Gertz's suit was part of a left-wing plot to frame the policeman and to discredit all law-enforcement agencies.

Gertz sued *American Opinion* for libel. The journal's defense was that Gertz was a public figure dealing with an issue of national interest. Based on the *Times v. Sullivan* outcome, the publishers of *American Opinion* said they were protected by the First Amendment. The Chicago court found

Gertz not to be a public figure, and the jury awarded him $50,000 in damages. On appeal, the judge overturned the ruling, explaining that while Gertz was neither a public official nor a public figure, he was involved in a public issue. Therefore, he could not charge libel, since he had not been able to prove "actual malice."

The case was eventually heard by the Supreme Court. The Court granted that Gertz was well known to those in his local community because of his legal work in civil liberty cases. They also noted that he was familiar to many in the legal profession as a writer for law journals. But, at the same time, they felt he was a private individual who had "achieved no general fame," nor was he a central figure in the public issue in question. He did not, therefore, need to prove "actual malice" in order to win a libel suit.

Libel remains a very thorny issue for advocates of free speech. At one extreme are the people who feel that there should be complete freedom in discussion of public affairs. These people say that since the Gertz case involved the public interest, the article in *American Opinion* should have been protected by the First Amendment. Champions of a very strict interpretation of the First Amendment go even further. Some favor eliminating all libel laws. All speech concerning public issues, they say, should be completely free of the risk of damage suits.

There is a trend, though, in the opposite direction, as shown in the case of Carol Burnett. The risk and fear of liability seems to be getting greater day by day. Some think it is shrinking or cutting down on discussion of people in the public eye. With so much money at stake, publishers are showing signs of becoming more cautious in the way they deal with public officials, public figures, and public affairs.

A recent Supreme Court ruling required journalists to describe their "state of mind" while writing a story. Although the intention in this case was to protect an individual against defamation, the result may be a further limit on protection of the press under the First Amendment. The effect could be to restrain very considerably the flow of information to the public.

Chapter Four

Espionage vs. National Security

In our state, naturally, there is and can be no place for freedom of speech, press, and so on for the foes of socialism." So wrote Andrei Vishinsky, the chief prosecutor of the Soviet Union, in his 1938 book, *The Law of the Soviet State*. By contrast, the First Amendment guarantees these very freedoms to all Americans, friends and foes of the government alike.

But even in a democracy there are limits. Some laws make it a crime to advocate the overthrow of the government by force. Other laws forbid the release of military and national security secrets. The problem is how to balance the people's right to express themselves, to criticize the government, and to be informed on national affairs, with the security of the state. This has been a major concern of Americans from the days of the original thirteen colonies through to the present.

Punishment After the Fact

In 1798, a mere nine years after the Bill of Rights was added to the Constitution, Congress passed the Sedition Act, a law that imposed fines and imprisonment on persons who openly criticized the government. It provided that:

If any person shall write, print, utter or publish . . . any false, scandalous and malicious writing or writings against the government . . . then such person . . . shall be punished by a fine not exceeding two thousand dollars, and by imprisonment not exceeding two years.

The chief aim of the law was to silence the opposition to President John Adams' ruling Federalist party. The Federalists were the party of the elite, who believed that the country should be governed by the wealthy landowners. Their opponents were the Democrat-Republicans, the party led by Thomas Jefferson, which placed much more faith in the common people. As a way of defeating Jefferson's bid for the presidency, the Federalists passed this bill forbidding any anti-government remarks.

The first victim of the Sedition Act was Congressman Matthew Lyon of Vermont. Lyon was born in Ireland, came to America as an indentured servant, and worked his way up until he became the publisher of a newspaper in Vermont. Lyon, in his paper, accused Adams of "an unbounded thirst for ridiculous pomp, foolish adulation, and selfish avarice."

In October 1798, Lyon was tried and found guilty of sedition. He was jailed but while in prison was reelected to Congress. The following February, a group of his friends collected enough money to pay his fine, and Lyon was released.

Eventually, the Sedition Act had the opposite effect to the one that was expected. The people and the press objected to it most strenuously and threw their support to Jefferson, electing him to office in 1800. The new president pardoned those convicted under the law and returned the fines they had paid. One year later, the Sedition Law expired.

For over a hundred years, no similar laws were enacted. But then World War I, and fear over the Communist Revolution in Russia, caused Congress to pass the Espionage Act of 1917. Espionage means spying, and the act forbade the publication of information "related to national defense," or the communication of such information to foreign agents. It also made it illegal to cause "insubordination in the Armed Forces or to interfere with the draft." A 1918 amendment extended it to include any "disloyal, profane, scurrilous, or abusive language about the form of government of the United States."

The 1917 law received its first challenge the year it was passed. A radical magazine, *The Masses*, printed articles against the war and the postmaster refused to allow the publication to be sent through the mails. A district court held that the statements made in *The Masses* were not criminal, since they did not directly urge the readers to take action against the war but only suggested it indirectly. On appeal, however, the postmaster's actions, as well as the constitutionality of the act, were upheld.

Another case involving this act reached the Supreme Court in 1919. The unanimous opinion affirmed the conviction of Charles Schenck, general secretary of the Socialist party, for violating the Espionage Act. Schenck had distributed 15,000 leaflets to potential draftees, denouncing the draft and urging them to refuse to serve. In his discussion of *Schenck v. United States*, Justice Oliver Wendell Holmes made two statements that established limits to the exercise of free speech. First he said: "The most stringent protection of free speech would not protect a man in falsely shouting fire in a theatre, and causing a panic." In other words, the courts should interfere with an individual's freedom of speech only when an immediate danger from such speech can be proved.

Justice Holmes then added: "The question in every case is whether the words used are used in such circumstances and are of such a nature as to create a clear and present danger that they will bring about the substantive evils that Congress has a right to prevent." The leaflet's call for resistance against the draft was found to be an example of just such a "clear and present danger," thereby justifying Schenck's conviction.

Many other very important Supreme Court decisions were handed down in similar cases during and following World War I. All grew out of the same conflict between the government's fear of subversion and its need for military and diplomatic secrecy, and the citizen's basic right to be informed and to be allowed to speak out freely.

With the onset of World War II, the same fears and conflicts were rekindled. In 1940, Congress passed the Smith Act, also called the Alien Registration Act. This law made it a crime to advocate the violent overthrow of the U.S. government, or to belong to a group that worked for that cause.

In 1951, while the United States and the Soviet Union were engaged in the Cold War, the Supreme Court upheld the Smith Act in the case of Eugene Dennis and ten other convicted leaders of the American Communist party. Chief Justice Fred M. Vinson spoke for the majority. He stated that "the overthrow of the Government by force and violence is certainly a substantial enough interest for the Government to limit speech."

Not everyone on the Court agreed. In a minority opinion, Justices Black and Douglas protested what they considered a weakening of the First Amendment. Justice Hugo Black said that the defendants "were not charged with overt acts of any kind designed to overthrow the Government. They were not even charged with saying anything or with writing anything designed to overthrow the Government." Their only guilt was planning "in the future to teach and advocate the forcible overthrow of the Government." Thus, Black concluded, "No matter how it is worded, this is a virulent form of prior censorship of speech and press, which I believe the First Amendment forbids."

In his dissent, Justice William O. Douglas presented his view that the defendants were not convicted because of their actions but because of their beliefs and thoughts. There is no criminal law, he said, that controls what a person is allowed to think.

A slight shift of position in the Supreme Court came in the 1969 case of *Brandenburg* v. *Ohio*. As a speaker at a Ku Klux Klan rally in Ohio, Brandenburg threatened that if the government "continues to suppress the white, Caucasian race," the Klan would march on Congress on the Fourth of

July, "400,000 strong." In a lower court he was convicted of advocating unlawful terrorism as a way of accomplishing his political goals.

The Supreme Court, though, reversed the conviction. It restated the test of punishable speech. The line, it said, should be drawn only against speech that advocates lawless action when it is also *likely* to lead to such action. The Justices, in this way, emphasized the legal distinction between ideas and action.

Prior Restraint

Most everyone agrees that in a free society people have the right to speak openly. For speech to be meaningful, it must be based on the free exchange of information and ideas. It follows, then, that freedom of speech depends on the public's knowing the facts that are necessary for intelligent decision-making. And citizens have the right to be told as much as possible about decisions made by government officials.

But what happens in times of war? What about military and national defense information that could cause great harm if it fell into enemy hands?

During a war, or in a major emergency declared by the president or the secretary of defense, the armed forces have a plan to establish censorship of all written and verbal communication from members of the armed forces. This plan has two basic objectives:

> *Prevent the disclosure of information which might assist the enemy, or adversely affect any policy of the United States. Collect and disseminate information which may assist the United States and its allies in the successful prosecution of a war.*

Each commander is responsible for setting up the censorship procedure, usually under the orders of the intelligence or security division of that unit.

The Pentagon has prepared a list of topics that are to be censored: information that might benefit the enemy or hurt the

United States; false military information; information about an escape from the enemy; and all personal communications to the enemy or people in enemy-occupied territory.

There is little question of the necessity for wartime censorship. Byron Price, Director of the U.S. Censorship Office during World War II, called it "a necessary evil." There is, however, more disagreement on the government's right to conduct diplomatic negotiations and conclude treaties with other nations without informing the public.

Some government leaders insist that no country can enter into arrangements with other countries without keeping some aspects of their work secret. But there are also libertarians who hold that the government is the servant of the people, and therefore the people have a basic right to know of all major policy decisions taken by their government.

A number of court cases have been heard on the issue of government secrecy versus disclosure. The outcomes are significant because they involve the principle of prior restraint, the most powerful form of censorship. The most important case to date involving prior restraint and the security of the state came in 1971, in *The New York Times v. United States*, otherwise known as the Pentagon Papers case.

At the heart of the issue were the Pentagon Papers, a 7,000-page document prepared by the Defense Department that described in great detail U.S. involvement in the Vietnam conflict. The government had classified the report "Top Secret" shortly after it was completed on January 15, 1969.

Daniel Ellsberg, a consultant to the Rand Corporation, a private research organization, had access to a copy of the Pentagon Papers. He discovered that the study contained information on the conduct of the war in Vietnam that he felt the Congress and the American public had the right to know. His attempts to interest several members of Congress in the report were unsuccessful. He therefore decided to duplicate parts of the document and make them available to *The New York Times* for publication.

On June 13, 1971, the *Times* printed the first excerpt. The following day, U.S. Attorney General John N. Mitchell asked

Daniel Ellsberg on August 16, 1971, about to appear before a Los Angeles federal court to enter his plea of "not guilty" for his action in turning over to *The New York Times* the so-called Pentagon Papers.

the newspaper to return the document and halt publication of the series. The *Times* refused. Two days later, after the third article was printed, the government obtained an order that stopped publication. The case went to court.

The government lawyers argued that disclosure would harm the defense and diplomatic interests of the United States. Representatives of the press said that the report dealt with historical facts that the public had a right to read and to know. On June 30, the Supreme Court, in a 6 to 3 decision, upheld the *Times'* right to publish, and the Pentagon Papers appeared in the press and in book form.

The outcome is considered important for striking down the doctrine of prior restraint. The judges who wrote the opinion felt that the material was not damaging to the national interest. They also claimed that the government had not proved "direct, immediate and irreparable damage to our nation or its people."

A few years later, in 1974, the Supreme Court unanimously decided that President Richard M. Nixon could not withhold release of the White House tapes needed as evidence in the Watergate break-in case. The president claimed he did not have to comply because of "executive privilege." The Court said that without "a claim of need to protect military, diplomatic or sensitive national security secrets," there was no justification for withholding even private presidential communications. Twelve days later, Nixon released three of the tapes he had sought to hide. Shortly after that he was forced to resign from office.

Exactly five years after the Supreme Court decision on the Pentagon Papers, the Court heard another prior restraint case. The state of Nebraska, in an effort to assure fair trials, passed a law limiting the right of newspapers to publish information on defendants in criminal trials. In the case known as *Nebraska Press Association v. Stuart*, the Supreme Court declared the law unconstitutional.

Then, in 1979, *The Progressive* magazine announced plans to publish an article entitled "The H-Bomb Secret," which was to include detailed plans for making a hydrogen bomb. The author claimed that he got the information from printed books and journals, conversations with scientists, and a public tour of a nuclear plant. The government insisted the information was secret, and that disclosure would help other nations build their own bombs. Thus they were able to obtain a court order forbidding publication. But while the case was in court, a newspaper reporter wrote a piece that contained essentially the same information. He had learned it all in six days of research at the Milwaukee Public Library. The government dropped its suit.

Over the years, most efforts at censorship through prior restraint have been struck down, either in the initial trial or on appeal. Nevertheless, the conflict between government control of classified material and public access to information is expected to continue. Such a struggle, it seems, is in the best tradition of a democratic society.

International Censorship

Every nation in the world has its own views on what its newspapers may publish and what its citizens have a right to know. Some countries have few controls on the press, and every effort to impose censorship is vigorously opposed. Other governments maintain a tight watch over public information, and only views that agree with official government policy are allowed to be printed.

Over the last few years, though, there has been, for the first time, an effort to impose press censorship on all the countries of the world. Most of the support for such international control comes from the Third World nations. These are the less-developed countries of the world that are not allied with either the Western democracies or the Eastern Communist states. Most of them practice some degree of press censorship in their own lands.

The opposition comes largely from the Western nations. They have a tradition of freedom of the press and believe in the free flow of information. Usually the Communist bloc countries back the Third World position.

The battle over international press censorship is being

waged mostly within one of the specialized agencies of the United Nations, the United Nations Educational, Scientific and Cultural Organization (UNESCO). UNESCO was created with the goal of promoting better understanding among the countries of the world by raising the educational levels of all people, by encouraging the development of science, and by arranging for cultural exchanges between nations.

The issue that is being debated in UNESCO between the Third World nations and the Western democracies has to do with the so-called "new world information order." This proposal grows out of the claim of the poorer nations that they are unfairly treated by the world's news media. They say that newspapers in the West, in particular, pay more attention to their countries' revolutions and coups, terrorism and starvation, floods and droughts, and other types of "negative" news, than they do to the positive gains and advances in their lands. The "new order" that they are asking for would let UNESCO decide what the world should be told about conditions in their countries and about the lives led by their people.

At every UNESCO conference since 1974, the Third World group has proposed various measures giving UNESCO the power to control the world press. Usually, the representatives of the Communist countries have sided with the Third World. The democracies are in opposition.

The West has almost always succeeded in defeating the most offensive parts of Third World proposals. However, they have been forced to make some compromises along the way. Observers are saying now that each struggle has left those who favor press control in a slightly better position than before.

One of the biggest victories for the "new order" was the virtual acceptance at the 1980 conference of UNESCO's right to set press standards for the world. Even though no actual rules were set, it marked the first time that independent nations considered allowing control of their newspapers by an international organization.

DICTATORIAL GOVERNMENTS
UN
FREEDOM OF THE PRESS
Blaine THE SPECTATOR

From the West's point of view, once UNESCO has the power to decide on media practices in each country, it will be able to hold back the flow of information. In the long run, they fear, this will encourage the spread of oppression. Nations that jail or torture their citizens for holding differing political or religious views try very hard to keep such information secret. They are afraid of public opinion, both within the country and outside of it. If newspapers are prevented from writing about such practices, it makes it easier for the offending nations to continue whatever they are doing.

Another outcome of the 1980 conference was the passage of a package of programs, including one to help the Palestine Liberation Organization and other revolutionary groups to spread their propaganda. Another suggested a study of journalistic "responsibility," and also formed a committee to research the "protection" of newspaper reporters around the world. According to many observers, the main purpose of these proposals is to lead up to the licensing of reporters. Those who accept the government's position in the country they are covering would get "safe-conduct" passes. Those against the government would not. In the West's eyes, such arrangements clash with the basic idea of a free press.

Until now, several of the Western countries have been donating communications equipment and training the operators of the communications agencies in Third World countries. Now it is proposed that these programs come under the direct control of UNESCO, instead of the donor countries.

Americans are in conflict over what the U.S. reaction to this situation should be. Should the United States continue to fight for freedom of the press in UNESCO, even in the face of the drift toward worldwide control?

There are those who agree that the Third World nations are at times unfairly treated by the world's news media. They think that proposals should be made and ways should be found to report on these nations in a more balanced manner. But most are strongly opposed to press control as the way to insure favorable reporting. And they feel that if matters keep moving in the same direction, the West may be forced to make more compromises. Eventually, it may be outvoted. Then, the Third World could succeed in making UNESCO the international censor of the world's media.

Should the United States withdraw from UNESCO as a way of protesting the emerging control policy? Such a move, while it might have certain advantages, also has its drawbacks. By removing itself from UNESCO, the United States would be giving up its role as leader of the opposition to the "new order." It would also leave its advocates free to institute any regulations they saw fit.

The controversy over international press censorship rages on, both in UNESCO and within many of the governments of the world. All who care deeply about the issue of censorship eagerly await the outcome.

Chapter Five

Pornography in Entertainment vs. Community Standards

The control of public entertainment, particularly of theatrical productions, dates far back in history. In ancient Rome, the Theodosian and Justinian codes established the rules for presenting drama. During the Middle Ages, the actors and playwrights, not having a place in the feudal system, came under the supervision of the church.

Starting in 1545, any play given in England had to be approved by the Master of the King's Revels. This office was replaced by that of the Lord Chamberlain in 1624. Under this censorship arrangement, actors were arrested for appearing in well-known classics, including Ben Jonson's *Volpone* and William Congreve's *Love for Love*. In more recent times, the Lord Chamberlain banned such plays as *The Rose Tattoo* by Tennessee Williams and *A View from the Bridge* by Arthur Miller.

Less censorship of live theater exists in the United States. In general, censors show more interest in new and emerging forms of entertainment, than in the older, established ones. In the United States, the chief object of censorship is the motion picture, or movie.

Movies are an important form of entertainment, but they also spread information. They make people think about issues in a new way, awaken them to fresh ideas, and bring them into contact with individuals in different life situations. Movies influence society as much as any other art. Because of the great power of films, many religious, educational, parent, and political organizations in our nation have tried to censor and influence their content.

History of Movie Censorship

The first motion picture theater opened in Los Angeles in 1902. It offered one hour of screen entertainment for a dime. Three years later, Harry Davis, a real estate operator, started the first "Nickelodeon." For only a nickel a person could watch a twenty-minute picture, with live piano accompaniment. From 1905 to 1907, 5,000 nickelodeons opened around the country.

With the commercial success of the nickelodeons, and an increased audience for motion pictures, came the first laws giving censors the power to see films before they were shown in public theaters. It also gave them the privilege to decide whether or not the films were morally suitable.

The first prior restraint censorship regulation of motion pictures was adopted by the lawmakers of the city of Chicago in 1907. In 1909, New York City made its own arrangements for reviewing films before they were released to the theaters. Other cities soon followed. The earliest state movie censorship board was installed in Pennsylvania in 1911. Soon after, Ohio and Kansas set up similar systems, and before much longer many states had their own licensing arrangements.

In the early days of film, most directors and producers went along with the state boards of censorship. They believed that getting the official approval of a state agency would prevent local groups within the states from interfering with the distribution of their pictures. But the censor boards charged review and licensing fees. As the costs mounted, the movie industry decided to challenge the system.

The first case taken to the U.S. Supreme Court was in 1915. The Mutual Film Corporation, a film distributor, charged that the censorship boards denied motion pictures the First Amendment right of a free press. In arguing the case, their lawyers said that licensing movies before they could be shown was prior restraint, and therefore illegal.

In a historic ruling, the Supreme Court said: "The exhibition of moving pictures is a business pure and simple . . . not to be regarded . . . as a part of the press of the country or as organs of public opinion." That is to say, movies are only entertainment, and as such they are not the same as newspapers or books and are thus not subject to the protection of the First Amendment.

This decision encouraged more states to set up film censorship boards. Many passed laws that imposed severe restraints on the fast-growing motion picture industry. The New York State law was typical. It declared that a film was eligible for a license "unless such film or a part hereof is obscene, indecent, immoral, inhuman, sacrilegious or is of such character that its exhibition would tend to corrupt morals or incite to crime." Almost everywhere, the decision of whether or not films could be shown was being made by state appointed review boards made up of censors with varying qualifications.

During the 1920s, sound movies, called talkies, were starting to be made. They triggered an increase in public concern about the moral level of the movies. In addition, gossip and scandals about the Hollywood stars further offended some members of the public.

The movie industry leaders decided in 1930 to counteract the bad publicity and growing local censorship by forming their own policing organization. It was known as the Production Code Administration. Since Will H. Hays, postmaster general of the United States at the time, was asked to become chairman, it was referred to as the Hays Office.

The Production Code established three basic principles. First, no film should lower the moral standards of the audience. This meant that the viewer's sympathy should never be attracted to the side of crime, evil, or sin. Second, all films should portray proper and correct standards of life. And finally, laws and rules should not be held up to ridicule or contempt. A number of specific guides were added that restricted nudity, profanity, drug use, talk of abortion, use of guns, or couples in bed.

Only those films that met the standards of the Production Code received the "seal" of approval. The seal allowed the film to be exhibited in all those theaters that had agreed to show code-approved films only. When films did not meet the seal's requirements, Hays suggested how they could be changed to conform to the code. If the producer followed the suggestions, the film was then granted the seal. If not, the movie was not distributed, since almost no theater in America would show it.

This tight control of the American movie industry continued through the 1930s and 1940s. Every film had to win the Production Code seal first, then pass the state and city censor boards. A still further hurdle was to earn the approval of the Legion of Decency, an organization set up in 1934 by the Catholic Church to monitor films for church members.

Action by the Courts

On December 12, 1950, an Italian film, *The Miracle,* opened at the Paris Theatre in New York City under a license granted by the New York State licensing board. The story tells of a simple-minded, unmarried woman goatherd who is made pregnant by a bearded stranger passing through the town. In her strong religious faith, the woman becomes convinced that the stranger was St. Joseph. The rest of the film deals with the cruelty of the townspeople, the trials the woman has to go through to have her baby, and ultimately the woman's victory over insanity.

Twelve days after it opened in New York City, the commissioner of licenses informed the theater that the film was "blasphemous," and that the theater's license would be suspended if showings were not stopped. At first, the film was withdrawn, but the commissioner's ruling was challenged in court. It was decided that the license commissioner did not have the authority to stop the showing of a film he disliked.

Performances started again, though the Legion of Decency, many Catholic leaders, and a number of private citizens protested strenuously. A three-man committee of the New York State Board of Regents reviewed the film, calling it "sacrilegious," and revoked its license. Joseph Burstyn, the distributor of *The Miracle*, sued the board for exceeding its authority. The case of *Joseph Burstyn, Inc. v. Wilson* passed through the state courts and on to the Supreme Court.

The Supreme Court made its ruling on May 26, 1952. It said that movies are "a significant medium for the communication of ideas," thereby striking down the Mutual Film Corporation doctrine and giving motion pictures the full protection of the First Amendment. The Court went on to say that "a state may not ban a film on the basis of a censor's conclusion that it is 'sacrilegious.'" The New York ban, therefore, was lifted.

Following this clear statement that movies are part of a free press, the local censorship boards could no longer deny a license because they thought the film might offend the views of community members. Although state boards of censors did not vanish at once, they did disappear gradually. The last one, the Maryland Board of Censors, broke up as recently as June 1981, sixty-five years after its founding.

In a 1959 decision on the film *Lady Chatterley's Lover*, the Supreme Court overturned a ruling of the New York State censors, who had denied a license to the film because it portrayed adultery "as a desirable, acceptable and proper pattern of behavior." In presenting the Court's majority opinion, Justice Potter Stewart said that such a portrayal was protected by freedom of speech:

> *What New York has done, therefore, is to prevent the exhibition of a motion picture because that picture advocates an idea—that adultery under certain circumstances may be proper behavior. Yet the First Amendment's basic guarantee is of freedom to advocate ideas. The state, quite simply, has struck at the very heart of constitutionally protected liberty.*

A unanimous Supreme Court decision delivered in 1965 effectively ended the practice of movie censorship. In the case, *Freedman v. Maryland*, a Baltimore theater manager, Ronald Freedman, challenged his conviction for violating Maryland law by showing the motion picture *Revenge at Daybreak* without a license from the state Board of Censors. While the Court ruling did not prohibit prior restraint in so many words, it did place on the censors the burden of proving that a film should not be shown. This made it close to impossible for any state or local movie censor to exercise any control over films exhibited in their jurisdiction.

The Industry's Position

At the same time as the censorship boards were being cut back by the courts, the film industry's Production Code was also under attack. Otto Preminger's 1953 movie, *The Moon Is Blue*, contributed to the collapse of the code. To earn the seal of approval for the movie, Preminger was told he would have to cut a sentence in which someone is called "a professional virgin." Preminger refused and did not get the seal. But even without it, he was able to distribute the film and turn a nice profit. His success pointed up the extent to which the Production Code had lost its power.

With the passing of the old code, the film industry feared that the government might step in and create a national censorship board. In 1956 and again in 1961, the Production Code was revised. But by 1968, it was clear that a completely new approach was needed.

Three organizations of the motion picture industry—the Motion Picture Association of America, the National Association of Theatre Owners, and the International Film Importers and Distributors of America—joined together to create a voluntary system they called the Classification and Rating Administration (CARA). CARA classifies films on the basis of their content, then grades them according to whether they are thought suitable to be seen by everybody or just by persons over a certain age. The organization's main purpose is to advise parents on the suitability of individual pictures for their children.

Richard D. Heffner, the chairman of CARA in 1981, made clear the distinction between the Hays Office and his group: "Some people consider us censors," he said. "We're not. We don't ban anything, or demand that changes be made in films. We don't make judgments about the value or quality of films. If you're over the age of 17, nothing we do affects what you can see in a movie theater."

While Heffner says, "There are no exact lists of inflexible dos and don'ts for each classification category," there are some general guidelines that CARA follows in arriving at its classifications: Theme—is it appropriate for young people? Language—would most parents prefer that their children not hear these words? Nudity—is it used in a way that is directly related to the plot? Sex—is it explicit or perverse? Violence—is it excessive?

The Rating Board is made up of six full-time, salaried adults, without any special background in motion pictures. Together they view two or three movies each day, placing them in the appropriate classification according to how each one feels "most parents" would react. A film can receive any one of four different ratings:

G: General audiences; all ages admitted. This film contains nothing in the view of the Rating Board that parents would find offensive for their younger children. The language, at most, goes little beyond polite conversation, there is no nudity or sex, and only a minimum of violence.

PG: Parental guidance suggested; some material may not be suitable for children. This classification means the film *may* contain material some parents consider unsuitable, and therefore should be investigated before sending or taking their children. There may be some profanity or violence. Sexual activity is not shown, but there may be brief nudity.

R: Restricted; anyone under 17 requires accompanying parent or guardian. This is considered an adult film in regard to theme, language, nudity, sex, or violence. The theme is mature, the language is strong, nudity is considerable, sexual activity is present, although not explicit, and the violence may be upsetting. An R rating is a strong signal that most parents will not consider it an appropriate film for young-

DENVER
PUBLIC LIBRARY
SEP 1983

sters. Any film that contains even one of the "harsher sexually derived words" automatically receives an R rating.

X: No one under 17 admitted. This film is most clearly only for adults. The rating can spring from sexual language, explicit sex, or brutal or sadistic violence. It does not mean that it is obscene or pornographic. Any number of high-quality, serious films have been given X ratings because they contained material most parents would have preferred their children not to see.

You may think that all producers would like their films to receive a rating of G. Not so. A number of outstanding pictures that have received G ratings have not been successful. Adults, who make up the bulk of the movie audience, have stayed away, assuming that they were "kiddie" pictures. Therefore, producers quite often will make changes in a G-rated film in the hope of having it rated PG, so that it will have a wider appeal.

CARA realizes that there are weaknesses in its rating system. Having only four very broad categories sometimes makes it difficult for parents to know whether or not a particular film is suitable for their children. Several alternate solutions are under consideration. One is to give the public the specific reasons for the classification of each movie. Another is to divide the R rating into R-13 for those over 13 years of age, and R-17, for those over 17.

The Catholic Church's historic concern about movies continues to the present. The Legion of Decency no longer exists. But the Office of Film and Broadcasting of the U.S. Catholic Conference has taken over many of its functions, including its system of film classification. These classifications and reviews of films, and of television programs as well, are based on the written opinions of a panel of priests, nuns, and lay Catholics. The reports are sent out to 120 Catholic newspapers with a readership of about four million.

The classification system is needed, explains coordinator Michael Gallagher, because many Church members have a stricter moral outlook than the average American parent. Further, the CARA ratings are not always enforced, and the categories of CARA are too vague, he says.

The Catholic Conference gives no recommendations. It just places each film in one of five categories. Each indicates whether a film is considered morally objectionable for a certain age group:

A-I Morally unobjectionable for general patronage.

A-II Morally unobjectionable for adults and adolescents.

A-III Morally unobjectionable for adults.

A-IV Morally unobjectionable for adults, but with reservations.

(This rating is used for movies of merit that might give the impression of being morally offensive.)

O Morally offensive

Along with the rating, a brief review of the film is included in the report.

Radio and TV

Each broadcasting network has an office of broadcast standards to keep an eye and ear on the content of shows being aired. The people in this office are responsible for the beep you hear when someone is about to use an off-color word in a talk show, or for the camera shift just as a couple enter into a passionate embrace in a romantic scene. This self-policing by the radio and TV industry was considered sufficient for many years. But more recently, certain problems have arisen.

One December afternoon in 1973, an independent radio station, WBAI in New York City, was broadcasting a program about the changes taking place in the American language. Comedian George Carlin, it was announced, would deliver a twelve-minute monologue dealing with seven words never before used on radio or TV. Before airing his talk, listeners were advised to shut off the radio or tune to another station if they thought they might find the language offensive.

In a humorous way, Carlin then proceeded to poke fun at the networks' policy of avoiding words dealing with sex, sexual organs, and human excrement. While he spoke, of course, Carlin used these words many times.

A man and his young son were riding in their car while the program was on the air. They heard the Carlin routine. Later, the father expressed his outrage in a letter of complaint to the Federal Communications Commission (FCC), the government agency that licenses radio and TV stations. The FCC investigated, and reprimanded WBAI for broadcasting "indecent language." It criticized the station especially for broadcasting the program in the afternoon, when children would very likely be among the listeners.

The owner of WBAI, the Pacifica Foundation, appealed the ruling to the Supreme Court. The Court found the monologue indecent and upheld the FCC's action. They agreed that the FCC did have the right to monitor broadcasts and take steps to prevent the airing of material that might offend the listeners.

Early in 1981, Reverend Donald E. Wildmon, a Methodist minister in Tupelo, Mississippi, announced the formation of a watchdog group called the Coalition for Better Television, made up of "scores of national organizations" and "thousands of local churches," according to its founder. Its purpose was to monitor TV shows to uncover those that contained "excessive and gratuitous sex and violence and profanity."

For three months, a team of about 4,000 volunteers around the country watched all of the prime-time TV series, noted their content and their sponsors. Reverend Wildmon collected the volunteers' reports and determined which sponsors were associated with the most objectionable shows. He threatened to organize a boycott of those sponsors' products by the groups in his coalition.

The advertisers became very uneasy. Proctor and Gamble, the biggest TV advertiser in the country, said it had already dropped fifty programs planned for the following season because they contained too much sex or violence. A number of other leading TV advertisers met with Reverend Wildmon to work out compromises on the proposed boycott.

By the end of June 1981, the Coalition for Better Television called off the threatened action. The boycott was unnecessary, Reverend Wildmon said, since so many advertisers had shown that they "basically share these same concerns." At the time, though, he warned that his group would continue to monitor the air waves. If the coalition finds objectionable programs on the air, it will launch the boycott.

The incident left unanswered the question: Is the Coalition for Better Television trying to impose censorship on the networks? A spokesperson for the coalition denied the charge. "All we're asking for," he said, "is a little balance in programming."

Everett Parker, head of the Office of Communication of the United Church of Christ, differs with this view. He says, "The coalition wants change through punishment." Like Parker, Peggy Charren, president of Action for Children's Television and a long-time critic of the networks, would like to change TV, but she does not like the tactics of the coalition. "We believe in improving television by expanding the numbers and types of programs, not by restricting programming," she says.

William Safire, the political columnist, views the situation in a different way. He affirms the right of the coalition to threaten a boycott. "The principle should be clear: Free speech includes the right to counter what others have the free speech to say." Whether you agree with the aim of the boycott or not, Safire says, "the weapon is in private hands, not government hands, and is thus free speech to be cherished, not deplored."

While the dispute over TV censorship goes on, everyone agrees that we are entering a new era of home entertainment. Cable TV is replacing the limited number of "broadcast" TV channels with literally hundreds of "narrowcast" programs, each one designed for a specific audience. Already there are "adult networks" and "adult programs" that offer explicit sex, excessive violence, and other features of hard-core pornography and X-rated movies.

This type of sexually oriented home entertainment is

proving immensely successful. About 60 percent of the ON TV subscription-television viewers in Chicago, Miami, and Phoenix, one study shows, are willing to pay additional money for late-night adult entertainment. The Qube cable television system in Columbus, Ohio, charges a separate fee for each movie seen. Pornographic films account for about half the total fees.

Similar services in Milwaukee attract 90 percent of the subscribers, and in Ann Arbor, Michigan, bring in 95 percent of all cable subscribers! What is more, there is a growing flood of video cassettes and disks available for home viewing. Industry sources guess that up to 50 percent of these are sexual in nature and would be X-rated if they were submitted to CARA.

The new technology is creating a fresh examination of censorship. What had been confined to sleazy bookstores and seedy theaters is now coming into millions of homes. People, while idly turning their TV channel selectors, can run across material they find revolting or offensive. Parents sometimes cannot prevent children from watching unsuitable shows without actually removing the TV set. How, then, can TV be restricted without violating the free speech guarantee of the First Amendment and the adults' freedom to see and hear whatever they want in the privacy of their homes?

Richard D. Heffner, chairman of CARA, fears the reactions of the American public. Anger at some of the material shown on cable TV may result in harsh and restrictive government censorship of the medium. This will not only "clean up" the objectionable shows but may also control and restrain the free expression of ideas.

The leaders of the cable and subscription TV industry, Professor Heffner believes, need to find ways to classify and categorize their programs. Parents require a sensible, practical way to control their children's viewing. Neither the broadcasters' nor the movie makers' current systems will fit this new industry. A novel approach must be devised. And it must be done quickly. If they wait too long, Professor Heffner fears, it may be too late.

Chapter Six

Repression vs. Student Rights

Do students have the right to wear buttons advocating political and social causes in school? Can they write anything they want in the student newspaper? Who decides what books go into the school library? Can parents choose the textbooks their children use? What should be done with racist or sexist children's books? Has the state the right to tell teachers what to teach their students?

Hundreds of court cases heard every year involve the rights of young people. Since 1969, some important changes have occurred in protecting students' liberties. Largely, they have come from cases tried according to the basic principles established by the Supreme Court decision in *Tinker v. Des Moines Independent School District.*

Freedom of Speech

The *Tinker* case began in the mid 1960s, a time of growing U.S. involvement in the Vietnam War. Large numbers of Americans were publicly expressing their antiwar feelings by wearing black armbands. This included thirteen-year-old Mary Beth Tinker, sixteen-year-old Christopher Eckhardt, and Mary Beth's brother, fifteen-year-old John. They decided

Mary Beth and John Tinker displaying the two black armbands that were the objects at issue in the Supreme Court case *Tinker v. Des Moines Independent School District.* Decided in favor of the students' right to show their beliefs symbolically, this late 1960s' case was considered a major victory for freedom of speech.

to wear the black cloth bands from December 16, 1965, until the end of the year.

When the students arrived at school on December 16, they were asked to remove the armbands. They refused and were suspended from school. Since they had only planned to wear the bands until January 1, they returned to school after New Year's Day without them. The authorities considered the incident closed. But Mary Beth and her brother, who had used the black bands to express their political opposition to the government's policies in Vietnam, felt that their rights had been violated. They took their case to court to establish the principle of freedom of "symbolic speech," such as wearing an armband or a political button.

The case went through the lower courts and finally reached the Supreme Court on February 24, 1969. Mary Beth and John Tinkers' lawyers argued that by not allowing the students to wear armbands, the school principal had abridged their right of free speech. School officials claimed that the school was no place for demonstrations, and that wearing the armbands might have led to a disturbance.

Justice Abe Fortas spoke for the majority in the 7 to 2 conclusion in favor of the Tinkers' position. Wearing the armband, he said,

> *was closely akin to 'pure speech,' which, we have repeatedly held, is entitled to comprehensive protection under the First Amendment. . . . It can hardly be argued that either students or teachers shed their constitutional rights to freedom of speech or expression at the school house gate. . . . They neither interrupted school activities nor sought to intrude in the school affairs or lives of others. They caused discussion outside of the classrooms, but no interference with work and no disorder.*

The decision established the principle that students' rights could be abridged only if the form of expression "materially disrupts classwork or involves substantial disorder or invasion of the rights of others."

A very strong dissent in this case was written by Justice Hugo L. Black. Justice Black foresaw that "it is nothing but wishful thinking to imagine that young, immature students will not soon believe it is their right to control the schools. . . ." His minority position reflected the widely held attitude that controlling student behavior in school is the responsibility of school authorities.

One public school official who shared Justice Black's view was Dr. Howard Hurwitz, former principal of Long Island City High School in New York City. Dr. Hurwitz was widely known as a very successful, although very strict, school head. In spite of the outcome in the *Tinker* case, Hurwitz felt it was up to him to exercise his authority in controlling behavior within his school.

In 1974, Priscilla Marco, a senior, wrote an article for the Long Island City High School student paper, *Skyline*, complaining that students were not properly informed of their rights. She insisted that *Skyline's* policy was shaped by Dr. Hurwitz and a faculty advisor, and not by the students who wrote for the paper. The principal called the article "irresponsible and badly written" and asked Priscilla to write it over again. She rewrote the article twice, but both times it was turned down.

Marco then took her case to Irving Anker, chancellor of the New York City school system. The chancellor ordered the principal to allow the article to be printed. He reasoned that the material neither disrupted classwork nor invaded the rights of others, which were the only constitutional reasons that allowed restraint on a student's speech. But Dr. Hurwitz resisted. It was his belief that he had the right to set the regulations for running his school.

At last, by printing its own edition of *Skyline*, which included Priscilla's article, the Board of Education forced Dr. Hurwitz to comply. Officials brought copies of the paper to the high school and distributed them to the students. By taking this action, the board asserted its power over school authorities, showing them that they must make certain that the constitutional rights of students are protected inside school as well as out.

The Right to Read

A high school principal in California bans five books written by Richard Brautigan because he thinks they might contain obscenities or offensive sexual references.

The librarian in a high school in Vermont is forced to resign because she fought the school board's decision to remove *The Wanderers* by Richard Price, and to restrict the use of *Carrie* by Stephen King and *Dog Day Afternoon* by Patrick Mann.

A group of nine adults charge into a high school library in Wisconsin, check out thirty-three books from a list they have with them, then lodge strong complaints with the school board about five of these books and five books they had checked out the previous year.

An Arizona school board restricts the circulation of *Two Queens of Heaven* by Doris Gates because they find the illustrations unsuitable for youngsters.

These cases are not at all unusual. In fact, they are typical of the challenges being leveled against school libraries today. Sometimes, the pressure to ban books in school comes from one or two people acting alone. Other times it comes from a group in the community. Often a school board demands that certain books be removed. In almost every instance, the effort to ban books is said to be justified by fear of the harmful effects that the books may have on young children.

A very famous book banning case began in March 1976. The Island Trees (New York) School Board removed nine, and later two more, "objectionable" books from the high school library. Among them were *Slaughterhouse-Five* by Kurt Vonnegut, *The Naked Ape* by Desmond Morris, *Down These Mean Streets* by Piri Thomas, *Black Boy* by Richard Wright, *Soul on Ice* by Eldridge Cleaver, and *Laughing Boy* by Oliver La Farge.

The board justified its action by calling the books "anti-American, anti-Christian, anti-Semitic, and just plain filthy." While the board members agreed such books might have a place in the public library, they felt they did not belong in the school library. They felt the board had "a moral obligation to protect the children in our schools from this moral danger."

Five students sued the school board on the grounds that this action had violated their rights under the First Amendment. Another nineteen public interest groups later joined in the court case to test the ban. The case, *Pico v. Board of Education, Island Trees Union Free School District No. 26*, passed through the courts until late 1981, when the U.S. Supreme Court said it would consider the matter at some future date. It is hoped that the decision by the highest court will finally set a clear precedent on school library book censorship.

Related to the Island Trees case is an incident that took place in Chelsea, Massachusetts, a working class city to the north of Boston. In May 1977, the school committee ordered the removal from the high school library of *Male and Female Under 18*. This book is an anthology of writings by a number of teenagers describing "what it is to be a girl or a boy growing up in the 1970s." Included is Jody Caravaglia's seventeen-line poem, "The City to a Young Girl," which deals with a young girl's experiences and emotions as she walks through the city's crowded streets.

When the poem was brought to the attention of Andrew Quigley, chairman of the school committee and publisher of the local paper, he found it "objectionable, salacious and obscene." He called a meeting of the school committee to consider the matter, distributing copies of the poem to the three male members of the committee but not to the three women, since he felt that the language was too "crude and offensive." In arguing for the ban, he said that the people of Chelsea were opposed to their children reading that kind of material: "To the average working-class Chelsea people this is dirty rotten filth." The board decided to rip the poem out of every copy of the book or remove the books from the library shelves.

Student leaders and the librarian, Sonja Coleman, put up a spirited defense of the book and the poem. They staunchly insisted on their right to read. Parents could decide if the book was suitable for their own children but had no right to deny it to other children, they said.

While waiting for the court to decide the merits of the case, the school committee voted unanimously to deny librarian Coleman a permanent tenured position. But Coleman brought suit, claiming that the school committee had violated an earlier court order forbidding any retaliation against the librarian. The committee then reversed itself and granted her tenure.

On July 5, 1978, federal judge Joseph Tauro ruled that the book and the poem were to remain on the school library shelves. He declared it unconstitutional for school committee members to censor books based on their own social or political views. School authorities may only move to suppress a book when it threatens "some substantial and legitimate government interest," Tauro said.

Those who favor censorship of school library books say that adults must have the right to exercise some control over what children read. In these times, they feel, unless responsible adults supervise youngsters' reading, they will be exposed to the worst kind of trash. At best this can cause offense; at worst it can result in emotional damage and even lead to antisocial behavior.

The anti-censorship group holds that youngsters in school have the same constitutional freedoms as everyone else, including the right to read whatever they want. It is only in this way, they claim, that children can develop the taste and understanding to distinguish between trash and serious literature. The country awaits a Supreme Court opinion on this vital issue.

The Right to Learn

An Indiana school board takes action that leads to the burning, in a public parking lot, of many copies of a textbook that deals with drugs and the sexual behavior of teenagers.

In South Carolina, parents protest the use of textbooks that teach their children about divorce and abortion.

Texas school authorities complain about a text that shows young Americans burning the American flag at a protest demonstration during the 1950s.

A New York school district rejects a textbook that shows

a Latino mother scrubbing floors, because it feels the picture stereotypes Latinos.

Right now, texts and other books used in the classroom are the center of a three-way controversy between the conservative right, the liberal left, and those concerned mostly with protecting First Amendment rights. Mel Gabler and his wife Norma, of Longview, Texas, are leading figures in the nation's textbook dispute. They have a very strong and active conservative position. The Gablers have been scrutinizing textbooks for about twenty years, ever since their sixteen-year-old son Jim complained to them that his high school history text made no mention of states' rights. Mel read the book and said that "what I saw set me on fire." In the text he found many instances of what he considered distortions of the truth. From that moment on, he says, he went on a crusade to monitor the country's textbooks. Joined by many others, he and Norma work to rid the schools of "undesirable texts" and to bring about "positive textbook reform."

In a 1978 article in *The Heritage Foundation,* the Gablers list some of the ideas they oppose: "Analysis of the personal and familial problems of the child; treating all moral questions as open, relative and debatable; evolution taught as fact; stories of violence, cruelty and morbidity presented as accurate portrayals of 'real life.'" The Gablers, in the same article, mention what they find lacking in most school texts: "Loyalty, faith, sacrifice and unselfishness; freedom and liberty; attachment to home and country; religious and cultural traditions; scientific evidence for creation."

Together with the seven staff members of their nonprofit organization, Educational Research Analysts, the Gablers review many textbooks each year. They then prepare reviews and comments that they submit to Texas education authorities. Their findings, though, are made available to other school boards, as well as to parent groups and individual parents around the country.

In a recent review, the Gablers cited Edgar Allan Poe's story "The Cask of Amontillado" as "not suitable" because of

THIS TEXTBOOK IS SOFT ON COMMUNISM!
WHAT'S COMMUNISM?
HISTORY

IT'S A TOTALITARIAN FORM OF GOVERNMENT THAT CONTROLS WHAT PEOPLE CAN READ AND...

...WON'T LET THEM THINK FOR THEMSELVES!
WHAT'RE YOU GOING TO DO ABOUT THE BOOK?
HISTORY
ROTHCO

BAN IT!
TAYLOR
ALBUQUERQUE TRIBUNE.

its "gruesome, murderous, bizarre content." They also think the story of Robin Hood is objectionable because it mentions stealing in an approving fashion. Among the issues that the group prefers not to see emphasized in texts are Watergate and the Vietnam conflict.

Mel Gabler sums up their position this way: "We believe that on all controversial issues, it's fair only if the student is given a balance to form an opinion. That's all we've asked for from the beginning: objectivity."

The Council on Interracial Books for Children (CIBC) and the National Organization for Women (NOW) are two major organizations that are also concerned with the content of textbooks and other books for children. But their point of view is quite different from that of the Gablers'.

CIBC and NOW want to eliminate racism, sexism, and other forms of bias from the books made available to children. They believe texts should deal with the contributions and careers of women, and the roles of blacks, Chicanos, American Indians, and immigrant groups in the development of the United States. The aged and the disabled, they say, should be portrayed free of distortion, prejudice, or stereotype. They should be seen as important groups in society that are capable of making significant contributions. "Children should learn, in their texts, the unpleasant truth about race and sex oppression, about national conquest, about poverty and other inequalities," says CIBC. "The fact that conflict is the likely result of oppression and inequalities should also be faced squarely."

In the guidelines they issue, CIBC cites several books for racism and sexism: *The Story of Doctor Doolittle* by Hugh Lofting, which "demeans Indians and Blacks"; P. L. Travers' *Mary Poppins,* which includes "racist illustrations"; and many fairy tales, such as *Hansel and Gretel,* which stereotype girls as "weak, helpless, foolish or passive." Most textbooks, they find, help promote racism and sexism by showing too few females, minorities, old people, and handicapped people, and by stereotyping human traits and activities.

CIBC and NOW find the legal justification for their

position in the Fourteenth Amendment, which guarantees "equal protection of the law" for everyone. If a book presents a poor image of some group of people, it deprives them of equal protection and may lead others to treat the group in a different way, which also violates the equal protection law. They also cite the Civil Rights Act of 1964. This law guarantees equal rights to all, forbidding discrimination in a number of specific areas on the basis of race, sex, or national origin. Books that show such bias are contributing to discrimination, they say, and are thus justly criticized.

Both CIBC and NOW say they oppose censorship, that this is not what they are doing. They tell how their activities differ from that of other textbook watchdog groups. By advocating an even wider *inclusion* of people, ideas, and events in books, they claim to reflect the plurality of American society. Other groups, they say, are mostly concerned with the *exclusion* of language, themes, and ideas that they find objectionable or undesirable.

Also, while people like the Gablers try to achieve their ends by banning books, as well as by preparing guidelines, CIBC and NOW mostly present their views in guidelines. Such services are intended to help others decide for themselves whether or not a book is racially or sexually biased.

The civil libertarians oppose *any* effort to curb the absolute freedoms to write and to read that are guaranteed by the Constitution. Most civil libertarians probably want to see an end to racial and sexual discrimination. But they insist that even if such an end is desirable, they are opposed to interfering, in any way, with the books used by children in school. They hold that there is no such thing as "good" censorship or "bad" censorship. In their view, all censorship is bad.

While the battle of the books rages on, another area of contention has arisen. Since the latter half of the nineteenth century, most scientists have accepted Charles Darwin's theory of evolution that humans are descended from a lower order of animals. In the view of some, though, Darwin's theory goes against the biblical description of the creation of humans.

The Scopes "monkey trial." Seated on the edge of the desk is Scopes' lawyer, Clarence Darrow. Directly behind him, leaning forward with arms crossed, is John T. Scopes.

In 1925, high school biology teacher John T. Scopes taught Darwin's theory of evolution. He wanted to test a Tennessee state law that forbade "any theory that denies the story of the divine creation of man as taught in the Bible." Scopes was found guilty and fined in a world-famous trial. An appeal to the state supreme court, however, acquitted Scopes on a technicality.

Despite the outcome of the Scopes' "monkey trial," as it was called, Darwin's theory has remained well established as a basis for teaching biology in school. But recently some new challenges to science education have been issued. A few organizations, with reputable scientists on their staffs, have called for the teaching of what they call "scientific creationism." In this view, humans were created by God in their present state and did not develop along the lines suggested by Darwin. By focusing on gaps in the fossil records of evolution and on some disputes among biologists, the creationists justify their demand for equal time in the school science curriculum.

Recent legislation has been passed and signed into law in Arkansas and Louisiana requiring the teaching of both theories, though the ruling was overturned in Arkansas by the state supreme court. In California, a superior court judge ruled that evolution must be taught as theory, not fact. And many other states have introduced legislation to give "scientific creationism" equal class time.

Now, some publishers are reviewing their treatment of evolution in their books. "We can't publish a book that doesn't recognize another point of view," admits one representative of a textbook company. But another says, "As long as the law marks the separation of religion and state, we will remain on our course, and we will not include creationism. If the law changes, we'll have to make critical decisions, but how many theories of creation are there that would have to be represented?"

There will likely be a court test of these laws soon. Perhaps then publishers and teachers will have some clear guidelines to help them resolve this conflict.

Chapter Seven

Censorship— For and Against

In every society there are people who are against censorship—its opponents—and those who are for censorship—its proponents. Both sides have arguments that they use to convince others of their point of view. Unfolding events also swing the public's attitude about censorship. A new president or Supreme Court Justice, or a change in the political climate, can cause the country's position on censorship to tilt in one direction or the other.

The debate for and against censorship centers around a few basic issues. In a democracy such as ours, it is important that everyone become familiar with these. Then, in a fair and open-minded way, each of us can arrive at his or her own position on censorship.

Constitutionality

One of the most basic questions about censorship has to do with its constitutionality. Does censorship violate First Amendment guarantees of free speech and a free press?

Judges, from local courts to the Supreme Court, seem firmly on the anti-censorship side. They have ruled again and again that the Constitution prohibits Congress from authorizing any form of censorship. The Fourteenth Amendment extends the same limitation to the states. Supreme Court Justice William O. Douglas said it in a few short words: "I think the First Amendment bars all kinds of censorship."

This same thought, that censorship laws are unconstitutional, rings out through many other court cases. Only when there is "a clear and present danger," said Justice Oliver Wendell Holmes, can there be restrictions on what a person writes or says. Censorship laws that magnify possible threats to our society may themselves be "instruments for dangerous abridgments of freedom of expression," remarked Justice Hugo L. Black on one occasion.

Under the Constitution, the right to speak and write freely includes the public's right to hear, to read, and to know, the anti-censorship people insist. Censorship becomes dangerous when it limits knowledge and cuts off the process of inquiry. Both are essential to a democracy.

The pro-censorship forces quote the First Amendment to make their point. The Amendment reads, "Congress shall make no law. . . ." It does not say, "There shall be no law. . . ." The meaning, they believe, is that the *federal* government is forbidden to establish a censorship system. It is not unconstitutional, however, for states and local communities to pass their own censorship laws.

The proponents also cite opinions of the Supreme Court to support their position that censorship laws are constitutional, and that the purpose of the First Amendment is not to protect obscenity and profanity. In the *Roth v. United States* case of 1957, Justice William J. Brennan, Jr., said that "Implicit in the history of the First Amendment is the rejection of obscenity . . . obscenity is not within the area of constitutionally protected speech or press." And again in the 1959 case of *Smith v. California*, Justice Felix Frankfurter said that "obscene speech and writings are not protected by the constitutional guarantees of freedom of speech and of the press."

Over the years, court opinions have changed regarding the constitutionality of various kinds of censorship. But all the recent decisions have supported the idea that censorship of obscenity is allowed under the Constitution. Therefore, those who believe in some form of censorship feel that the latest thinking among the nation's judges is swinging toward their point of view, which is that some degree of censorship is legal, valid, and necessary.

"Vague Is Void" Doctrine

Even if censorship of obscenity is approved by the courts, the anti-censorship forces protest, the laws are still illegal. The reason they give is that such laws are vague, inconsistent, and difficult to apply. When someone steals money, he or she knows that a law is being broken. But what if a person writes a book? How can he or she tell if it is offensive? If it lacks serious value? If it appeals to prurient interest? If it violates community standards?

Judge Sidney Goldman of the superior court of New Jersey once criticized the failure of judges and courts to set clear rules for censoring the written word: "Even the most cursory account of literary censorship will show its contradictions, the absence of valid standards, its lack of inner logic and outward consistency."

The American Civil Liberties Union made an even stronger statement about the vague definitions of the words obscenity and pornography: "They have no meanings other than in terms entirely individual and drawing on each person's religious and moral standards or concepts of good taste."

The censorship advocates do not accept this position. They reply that many legal terms are just as vague as the term obscenity. "Justifiable homicide," "simple negligence," "reasonable doubt," and "due process," are just as difficult to define as obscenity. Although these terms are not exact, they are clear enough for judges and juries to understand.

Censorship proponents say that people can use common sense and good taste to distinguish fine art from trash. They can tell the difference between excessive nudity and nudity used as part of a dramatic plot, and between explicit sex used

The News and Observer

ROTHCO

to arouse and sex portrayed for a serious artistic purpose. Justice Potter Stewart, at a time when Supreme Court Justices could not agree on a definition of obscenity, is reported to have said that, though he found it hard to define the word, "I know it when I see it." And that is just what many people believe.

Link to Violence

Those who oppose censorship maintain that there is no connection between obscenity and violence. They mention several research reports to support this argument. In the 1970 report of the President's Commission on Obscenity and Pornography, the conclusion was, "There is no evidence that exposure to pornography operates as a cause of misconduct in either youths or adults." Further, the Psychiatric Department of the Danish Council of Forensic Medicine reported: "No scientific experiment exists which can lay a basis for the assumption that pornography or 'obscene' pictures and films contribute to the committing of sexual offenses by normal adults or young people." In fact, when Denmark removed all anti-obscenity laws, the result was a decrease of 30 to 50 percent in the number of sex crimes, except for rape, which remained about the same.

A democratic society accepts that a person's freedoms are guaranteed as long as they do not interfere with the rights of others. On this basis, people should be able to buy and use obscene materials—if they are able to do so without subjecting the public to obscene displays of any kind. But to ban all obscene items just because they might produce antisocial thoughts, the opponents feel, is to exceed the power of government.

The proponents of censorship raise several other points. For example, they point out that even though the President's Commission found no link between pornography and misconduct, this conclusion was rejected both by President Richard M. Nixon and the U.S. Senate.

Also, some years ago, the founder and director of the FBI, J. Edgar Hoover, expressed the view that a cause-and-effect relationship exists between reading obscene books and committing antisocial acts. "I believe pornography is a major cause of sex violence," he said. Similar views have come from several distinguished professors of psychiatry and psychotherapists of various disciplines.

Just as the words and images of TV commercials lead people to buy a particular brand of soap, the words and images of obscenity and violence may also lead people to action. And this could be very dangerous to society, proponents of censorship say. In addition, the proponents suggest that even if 99 percent of the people are not affected, there should be censorship to avoid the damage that can be done by the one percent who are led to commit antisocial acts by what they see or read.

Difficult to Enforce

Evidence surrounds us that the present obscenity laws have not lessened the amount of material that so many find offensive. This raises some important questions. For example, is it possible to get rid of such materials by suppressing them? Don't obscenity laws make the items, like forbidden fruit, seem even sweeter?

Opponents of censorship say that labeling certain materials "sinful" does little to make them disappear. Violations of censorship laws are widespread. Anyone determined to use such materials will find them.

Some years ago, an advertising agency did a poll of teenagers. One of the questions was, what sales slogan most attracts your attention? The answer was, "Adults Only." If something is banned, and therefore hard to get, that makes it seem all the more desirable to some people. Thus, the restriction of censorship leads to the sale of more "dirty" books and magazines and the attendance of more patrons at pornographic movies—the very thing the proponents of censorship are trying to prevent.

The proponents reply that all laws are hard to enforce. Just because the present laws have not eliminated obscenity is no reason to toss them out. After all, other laws have not

"WHAT TRIGGERS ALL THIS VIOLENCE?"

eliminated robbery, rape, and murder, they say, and those laws remain on the books. What is needed are stronger efforts to enforce the law, and to pass any needed new legislation.

Does Censorship Work?

Justice Hugo L. Black once said, "Undoubtedly, a government policy of unfettered communication of ideas does entail dangers. To the Founders of this Nation, however, the benefits derived from free expression were worth the risk."

Those who are against censorship agree that not having censorship does not solve the problem of protecting people from material they find offensive. But they say it is less dangerous and causes less harm than censorship laws. If nothing else, strict laws foster the growth of a criminal class to produce and sell the banned items.

History disproves the claims of the anti-censorship forces, according to those who are pro-censorship. Take the continuing growth of the pornography industry, they say. Within the last generation, despite obscenity laws, entire sections of many cities have been taken over by shops and theaters that cater to the so-called sex trade. Many young children are drawn into this world, to pose for the pictures and act in the movies, in addition to being able to buy and see the material without difficulty.

For these reasons, many proponents think that the present policy, based on a strict, absolute reading of the First Amendment, has failed. They urge a more sensible, practical interpretation to protect society from these ills. They would like to see less concern with the rights of the dealers in obscenity and more thought for traditional American values.

In addition to the fundamental issues, both sides raise a number of other points.

The opponents of censorship say it is a violation of the Constitution to limit the freedom of adults to see and read what they want, in order to protect children from exposure to such materials. The proponents argue that even during times of the strictest censorship, those seeking pornography were able to find it, so there is no real violation of adults' rights.

Those opposed warn that under censorship laws, the creativity of the nation's great writers and artists is stifled. Those who favor censorship accept this as a possibility. But they hold that if the censorship is carefully planned and properly carried out, the danger is very remote. And further, even if some few works of fine art are censored, it is a small price to pay for protecting the public from some of the smut that is passed off as art.

Finally, the anti-censorship people claim that the way to get rid of obscenity and excessive violence is through moral pressure. If parents and religious leaders guide youngsters, if adults do not buy trashy books or magazines or watch pornographic movies or TV shows, they would soon fade away. Agreed, say those who favor censorship. But let's speed up the process by passing laws against this kind of material.

Both opponents and proponents of censorship believe that their position is right. They feel that reason is on their side. They argue in terms of what they think is best for their children, and for the society in which we live.

The opponents of censorship seek to prevent repression and erosion of basic rights by trying to convince others, taking private actions, and urging the passage of public laws. The proponents strive to limit the spread of materials they find offensive or objectionable by the same means. That there is room for these opposing points of view, and many opportunities for both to present their positions to the public, is a testament to the strength and vitality of our democratic form of government.

Glossary

Censorship. Control of communication by restricting what can be written, exhibited, or said.

Comstockery. Practicing censorship in a fanatical way.

Corrupt. To lower the moral level.

Defamation. An attack on someone's good name or reputation.

Evolution. The theory, first stated by Charles Darwin, that all species are descended from other species, including humans; accepted as fact by most scientists.

Explicit. Full and clear; leaving nothing hidden.

Heresy. Expression of ideas or beliefs different from the accepted doctrine.

Libel. Written defamation. (See Defamation.)

Moral. Following the accepted rules of correct conduct.

Obscene. Designed to cause impure sexual thoughts; lewd or sexually offensive.

Pornography. Material dealing with sex in a nonartistic way; from the Greek, meaning "to write about prostitutes."

Prurient. Having lustful sexual thoughts; from the Latin word meaning "itch."

Salacious. Indecent or obscene.

PRAIRIE MEDIA CENTER

Scientific creationism. The view that humans were created in their present form; based on the biblical account and some current scientific theories.

Sedition. Any writing, speech, or act that urges revolt against the government.

Slander. Spoken defamation. (See Defamation.)

Suppress. To control or put an end to certain activities.

Symbolic speech. Making a statement, such as expressing a political view, other than by speech or writing.

Suggested Reading

Of General Interest

Dworkin, Andrea. *Pornography*. New York: Putnam, 1981.

Friendly, Fred. *Minnesota Rag*. New York: Random House, 1981.

Griffin, Susan. *Pornography and Silence*. New York: Harper, 1981.

Hart, Harold H., ed. *Censorship: For and Against*. New York: Hart, 1971.

Lofton, John. *The Press as Guardian of the First Amendment*. Columbia, South Carolina: University of South Carolina, 1980.

Report of the Commission on Obscenity and Pornography. New York: Random House, 1970.

Against Censorship

Haiman, Franklyn S. *Freedom of Speech*. Skokie, Illinois: National Textbook, 1976.

Hentoff, Nat. *The First Freedom*. New York: Delacorte, 1980.

Rembar, Charles. *The End of Obscenity*. New York: Random House, 1968.

For Censorship

Clor, Harry M. *Obscenity and Public Morality*. Chicago: University of Chicago, 1969.

Gardiner, Harold, S. J. *Catholic Viewpoint on Censorship*. Garden City, New York: Doubleday, 1958.

Kilpatrick, James Jackson. *The Smut Peddlers*. Garden City, New York: Doubleday, 1960.

Index

PRAIRIE MEDIA CENTER

About the Author

Melvin Berger, author of over sixty books for young readers, was for many years a public school teacher before devoting full time to his writing. He is the author of a number of books for Franklin Watts, including *Bionics* in the Impact series and *Disastrous Volcanoes* and *Disastrous Floods and Tidal Waves* in the First Book series.

Mr. Berger is married to author Gilda Berger. They have two daughters and live in Great Neck, New York.